LEGENDS OF

MYTHICAL MONSTERS

CONTENTS

Written by Mike Rampton

Illustrated by Jennifer Beam

Collins

1 THE ANCIENT WORLD OF MYTHS

For all human history, people have loved storytelling. Every culture on Earth has some kind of storytelling tradition, both to entertain one another and to try and make sense of the world. This began long before there was any way of writing the stories down or recording them in any way.

Today we have different ways of enjoying stories, but our taste for tales of bravery, adventures and unbelievable events has remained the same since the days of early humans gathering around a fire to be entertained.

And what would the world of stories be without a few monsters, beasts and other odd creatures?

The modern world owes a lot to a period of time known as the **classical age**. Lasting from about 800 BCE to 500 CE, and centred first on ancient Greece, then ancient Rome (and a bit of ancient Egypt), this era saw massive changes in the world.

A lot of ideas that were formed during the classical age are still around today, including elements of language, law, science, schools and voting. While some of the ideas they had about science and medicine were inaccurate by our standards, the journey towards figuring an awful lot out began in the ancient world.

During this period, people also started collecting stories that had been told out loud for centuries and writing them down, and reinventing them when they did so.

A lot of stories from the ancient world – some even older than ancient Greece and Rome – came in the form of epic poems. These were incredibly long stories with a lot of parts and, before the development of writing, storytellers had to come up with clever ways to learn them off by heart.

Epic poems tend to follow heroic figures as they battle with incredibly powerful forces, very much like superhero movies do today. Nothing shows off how clever, brave and strong a hero is like going up against ludicrously powerful foes. But instead of getting their powers from technology, like a lot of modern heroes do, the heroes of epic poems got their powers from gods and magic.

THE MYTHMAKERS

A lot of our ancient stories come from a handful of works by writers in the ancient world, who wrote down stories that had been told aloud for a long time and built on the work of others that had come before them.

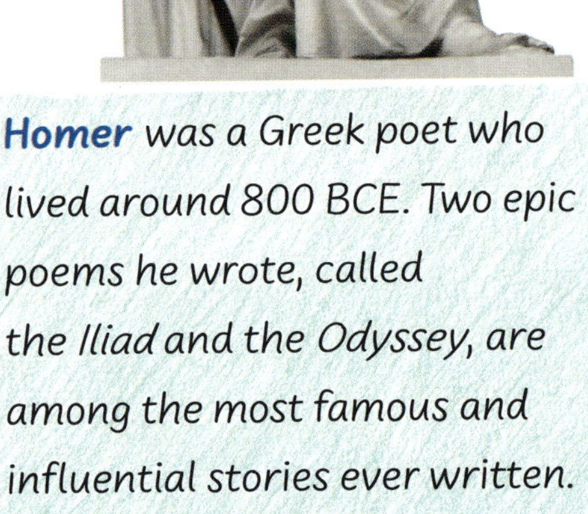

Homer *was a Greek poet who lived around 800 BCE. Two epic poems he wrote, called the* Iliad *and the* Odyssey, *are among the most famous and influential stories ever written.*

Virgil was a Roman poet who lived in the 1st century BCE. His three best-known works are all a bit tricky to say: the *Eclogues*, *Georgics* and *Aeneid*.

Ovid was another Roman poet, whose work, *Metamorphoses*, retold Greek myths for Roman audiences and later inspired the English playwright Shakespeare.

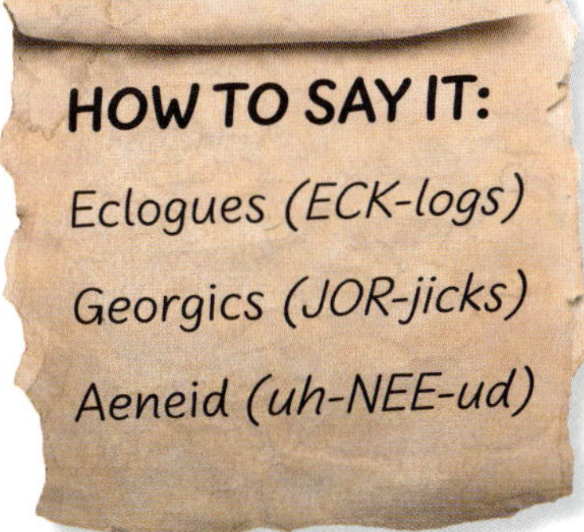

2 CYCLOPS AND THE GREAT EYE-DEA

The *Odyssey*, the epic poem by the ancient Greek author Homer, tells the long story of the legendary king Odysseus. One of the best-known adventures Odysseus had in the story was an encounter with a one-eyed giant known as a Cyclops.

This Cyclops, named Polyphemus, lived on an island with some others and worked as a shepherd. Odysseus and his men were hungry, and when they found the island, they sneaked into Polyphemus's cave and started eating his food.

HOW TO SAY IT:

Odyssey (ODD-uh-see)

Odysseus (oh-DISS-ee-us)

Polyphemus (po-luh-FEE-mus)

However, he came back and trapped them inside, eating a few of the sailors and telling them he would eat the rest. Odysseus had to come up with a plan. He talked to Polyphemus for hours, telling him his name was Nobody, until eventually Polyphemus fell asleep by the fire.

Odysseus and his remaining men then heated up a sharp stick in the fire and stabbed the sleeping Polyphemus in the eye with it. When he screamed, other giants called out to see what was happening, but Polyphemus shouted, "Nobody is hurting me!" so they left him alone.

In the morning, Polyphemus, unable to see, tried to let his sheep out while leaving the men trapped in the cave, so he felt every sheep's back as they walked out of the cave. However, Odysseus and his men had tied themselves to the sheep's stomachs, and got away.

A lot of myths involve people beating enemies much more powerful than them by using their wits and cunning. The idea of "brains over brawn", and intelligence being a better weapon than sheer strength, is a big part of all kinds of tales, from ancient myths to modern superhero stories.

There are several types of animal that have been named after the Cyclops. The Polyphemus moth gets its name from the eye-like pattern on its wings (although it has two wings, so maybe that isn't a particularly appropriate name). There's also a type of tortoise found in the United States, the gopher tortoise, (*Gopherus polyphemus*) that was named after him because it likes digging itself into caves.

Polyphemus moth

gopher tortoise

However, there is another animal connection that might actually be where the story originates. During the Pleistocene era (from 2.5 million years ago until around 12,000 years ago), the areas which are now Greece and Italy were home to small elephants. A few of their skulls have been found in the region, and if you've never seen an elephant and don't know about trunks, the big hole in the front of an elephant skull can easily be mistaken for an enormous eye …

3 GODS AND MONSTERS

In the ancient world, a lot of things that are now easily explained by science didn't seem to make sense. Ideas like gravity, or Earth revolving around the Sun, were yet to be properly understood, so they were explained with stories of gods and otherworldly beings instead. For instance, the Sun was said to be placed in a chariot by the sun god Helios, who then rode it across the sky; this was to explain the sun coming up and going down every day.

The ancient Greeks had a huge number of gods and goddesses, with extremely complicated family trees. Many of them would be killed and then come back to life, or spend time disguised as something else, and it all got very confusing. They were then given new names by the Romans, and had their stories rewritten, making the world of what is known as **Greco-Roman mythology** really hard to follow!

The ancient Greeks believed that the many gods and goddesses who watched over them lived on Mount Olympus, a palace in the clouds. They believed that storms were sent by angry gods, and that an army going into battle would have a much better chance with the gods on their side.

Some of these gods were more powerful than others, and a lot of them had specific areas of expertise.

Zeus
(king of the gods, more powerful than all the others)

Hera
(goddess of women)

You would pray to the relevant ones before doing anything you needed their help with.

However, as the stories go, a lot of the gods were quite badly behaved. They were prone to having arguments and playing tricks to get back at one another, or letting humans get caught up in their dramas …

As well as gods, the stories of the ancient world were filled with monsters. The underworld, where the ancient Greeks believed people went when they died, was said to be guarded by a monstrous dog, Cerberus. Different versions of the stories give Cerberus any number of heads from one to 50, often with multiple tongues in each one, and a snake for a tail.

Some monsters were said to have been created by angry gods, punishing humans for misbehaving. Or they were placed there as obstacles for heroes to beat to prove their worth.

And monsters would meet other monsters, and have baby monsters, more monstrous than the monsters they came from. Then they'd meet other monsters, and so on. The family tree of ancient mythical monsters changed with every telling of these stories, and was even more confusing than the gods' one!

4 THE A-MAZE-ING MINOTAUR

Another ancient tale which has lasting, modern-day effects is that of the half-man, half-bull known as the Minotaur.

The Minotaur's father, King Minos, trapped the Minotaur in the middle of an almost impossible maze, called the Labyrinth, to keep him out of sight. He arranged for young people to be sent into it to get lost, caught and eaten by his monstrous offspring.

A hero named Theseus (said to be half-god) volunteered to be one of those people, vowing to kill the Minotaur. King Minos's daughter Ariadne helped him, sneaking him a ball of string and a sword. Theseus went into the maze, unravelling the ball of string as he did so, and managed to kill the Minotaur. He then retraced his steps with the string and escaped.

While a lot of cultures independently came up with the idea of mazes, the legendary Labyrinth is arguably the best-known one. Over the centuries since, there have been several periods when people have got really into the classical world and recreating art, architecture and other elements from that era. In Renaissance times (the 15th and 16th centuries) it became popular in Europe for rich people to grow big mazes made from hedges to show off how fancy and enormous their gardens were. King Louis XIV of France had an enormous maze built in his palace at Versailles, which inspired King William III of England to have his own built at Hampton Court Palace near London, which you can still visit today.

In North America, mazes cut out of corn fields are popular every autumn. And, of course, two-dimensional mazes can be found in puzzle books everywhere.

the Hampton Court Palace maze

5 MIXED-UP MONSTERS

Storytelling is sometimes about shortcuts.

Take the Minotaur from Chapter 4 – that's a difficult creature to describe if you can't compare it to a man or a bull, but easy if you can. Half-man, half-bull: simple!

A lot of the monsters that have stood the test of time are hybrids: part one thing, part another. Through a lot of history most people couldn't read or write, so rather than books, stories were passed down through generations by being spoken out loud (known as the "oral tradition"). The easier it was to get a vivid idea across in a few words, the better.

Pegasus (horse + wings) was born from the blood of Medusa (see Chapter 6) and, among other things, is said to have helped Zeus (the Greek god of thunder) carry thunderbolts.

The **Chimera** (lion + goat + snake + dragon) had a lot going on – it was a whole lion, with the top of a goat sticking out of its back, and a snake for a tail (complete with head). Oh, and dragon's wings. And it breathed fire, from the goat's mouth. The name "chimera" has since been used in modern science, often referring to some sort of genetic mix taking place.

A **Hippocampus** (horse + fish) turned up in some myths pulling the chariot of Poseidon, god of the sea. It had the upper body of a horse and the lower body of a fish, and in some pictures was shown with wings. The name "hippocampus" is now used to name the group of creatures that seahorses are in. There are also hippocampi in your brain – a part of the brain to do with memory that looks surprisingly seahorse-like.

Centaurs *(person + horse) had the top half of humans and the legs and lower bodies of horses. There are thoughts that the idea of centaurs might have come from groups of people who had never seen horses before being visited by horseriding soldiers and thinking they were one creature.*

*The **Sphinx** (person + lion + eagle) had a woman's head, a lion's body and an eagle's wings, and would deviously give people an unsolvable riddle. When they failed to solve it, she would eat them. The Sphinx changed slightly when it became part of ancient Egyptian culture – the statue of one in Giza in Egypt is male, has no wings and is presented as kind. The idea of "the riddle of the Sphinx" is still used to describe really tricky problems.*

6 MEDUSA'S BAD HAIR DAY

Another hero who had a lot of stories told about him was Perseus, said to be the half-human son of Zeus. He was sent to kill Medusa, one of three Gorgons. The Gorgons were women with snakes for hair and sharp claws, who turned anyone who looked at them to stone.

Perseus was helped out by two of Zeus's other children – the messenger god Hermes gave him a sword, an invisibility helmet and winged shoes so he could fly, while Athena the goddess of wisdom gave him a shiny shield and a special bag.

After tracking down the Gorgons, Perseus was able to get close enough to them by walking backwards and looking at their reflection in his shield. He cut Medusa's head off, then made himself invisible and flew away with it hidden in the special bag.

Medusa's severed head was later used as a weapon to turn people into stone.

There are ancient myths of people being turned into stone from all over the world, often associated with peculiar human-shaped rock formations or mysterious prehistoric monuments, but the story of Medusa is arguably the most famous.

The idea of deliberately turning people into stone, or petrifying them, showed up later in all sorts of stories – it happens in the Narnia books, Harry Potter and *The Lord of the Rings*. Some of the most famous artists in history, including Leonardo da Vinci, Caravaggio and Picasso, have painted Medusa.

"Medusa" by Caravaggio

7 BAD THINGS HAPPEN AT SEA

In the ancient world, the sea was incredibly important. Sailing was essential for trading with other countries, exploring new places and gathering wealth. A lot of the heroes of ancient Greek stories were sailors. For many people in ancient times, the sea was huge and mysterious. It seemed totally possible that, after a few weeks of sailing, you might find an island populated by giants, or unthinkably enormous sea monsters.

Sailors would often come back from voyages with incredible stories of the creatures they'd seen out at sea. There were a few reasons for this. Being at sea is exhausting, and tired eyes are more likely to mistake one thing for another. Sailors also went out expecting to see all sorts of unexpected things due to the stories they had heard. And, because of that, they were maybe a bit more likely to exaggerate about what they'd seen, or make things up entirely …

Many of the watery creatures described by sailors seem implausible to us, but made sense to people at the time, as the ocean held such mystery.

Sirens *were first described in ancient Greece as birds with the heads of women who were said to sing so beautifully that sailors would follow their voices and end up crashing into rocks. Over the centuries, descriptions and pictures of these creatures evolved, until they became less birdlike, more fish-like, and became named … mermaids.*

The **Hydra** was a lake monster – like a sea monster but in a lake – with a lot of heads. Some stories told of the Hydra growing back two heads for every one that was cut off. It also had poisonous breath and toxic blood. Lots of things have been named after this monster, from tiny creatures with lots of heads to all sorts of other fictional monsters.

Cetus *was a word used to describe various sea monsters. The word for the biological group that whales are part of – cetaceans – is inspired by Cetus monsters. There are a few ancient depictions of them that look particularly strange. Some historians believe that the ancient Greeks found skulls of long-extinct giraffes that once inhabited the Greek islands and assumed they must be sea monsters.*

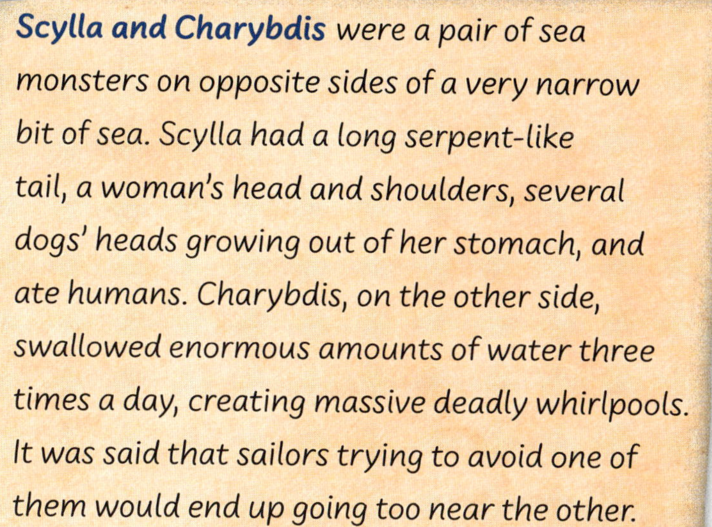

Scylla and Charybdis *were a pair of sea monsters on opposite sides of a very narrow bit of sea. Scylla had a long serpent-like tail, a woman's head and shoulders, several dogs' heads growing out of her stomach, and ate humans. Charybdis, on the other side, swallowed enormous amounts of water three times a day, creating massive deadly whirlpools. It was said that sailors trying to avoid one of them would end up going too near the other.*

8 THE MYTHS THAT WON'T DIE

Stories from the ancient world were constantly reinvented and played with by generation after generation of storytellers, and we're still enjoying and adapting them today. There are monsters and other mythical creatures from thousands of years ago that pop up in new stories all the time.

Some of the stories have their foundation in real-life fossils, science that wasn't understood at the time. Others have gone the opposite way and shaped modern science. The history of monsters and myths is always twisting and turning, adapting and inspiring, and will continue to do so for centuries, creating stories to be enjoyed for years to come.

GLOSSARY

classical age the period from around 800 BCE to AD 500 in ancient Greece and Rome

Greco-Roman mythology the combined gods and mythical creatures of the ancient Greeks and Romans

INDEX

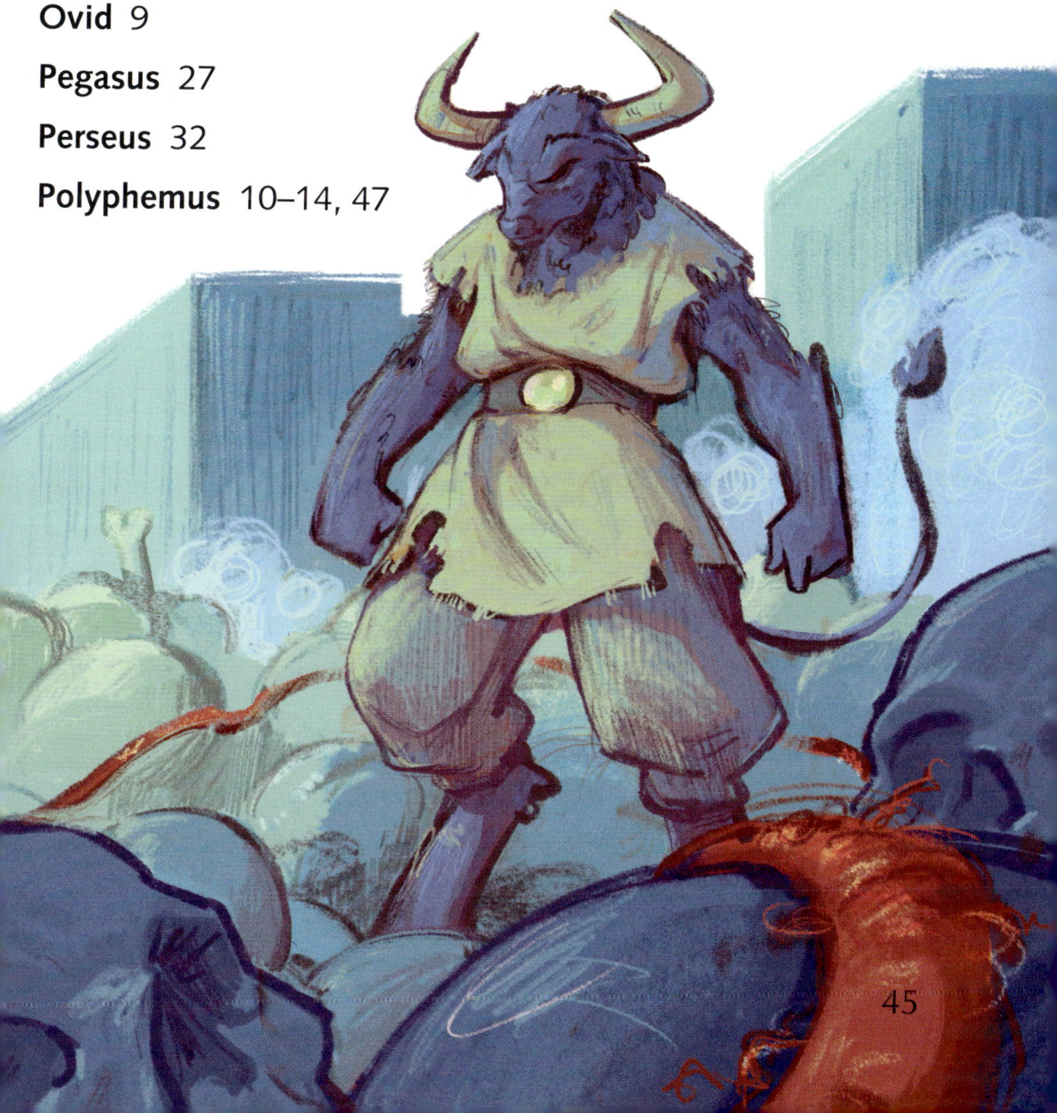

HOW REAL LIFE INSPIRES MYTH ...

mysterious elephant skulls

the Cyclops myth

the Sun rising every day

Helios and his chariot

soldiers on horseback → Centaurs

... AND MYTH INSPIRES SCIENCE

the Hippocampus
(the mythical creature)

the hippocampus
(within the brain)

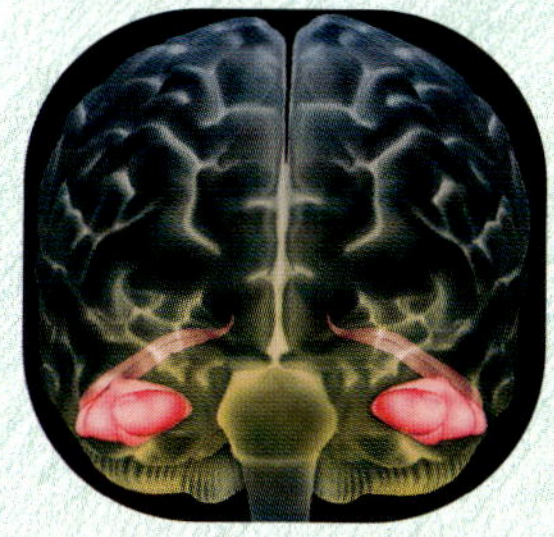

Cyclops

the Polyphemus moth

the Chimera
(the mythical creature)

scientific chimeras

Ideas for reading

Written by Gill Matthews
Primary Literacy Consultant

Reading objectives:

- check that the text makes sense to them, discuss their understanding and explain the meaning of words in context
- ask questions to improve their understanding of a text
- identify main ideas drawn from more than one paragraph and summarise these
- retrieve and record information from non-fiction

Spoken language objectives:

- use relevant strategies to build their vocabulary
- articulate and justify answers, arguments and opinions
- participate in discussions, presentations, performances, role play, improvisations and debates

Curriculum links: History: ancient Greece

Interest words: unbelievable, inaccurate, incredibly, ludicrously, influential

Build a context for reading

- Ask children to look closely at the front cover and to read the title. Explore their knowledge and understanding of myths. Ask whether they can identify any of the creatures on the cover.
- Read the back-cover blurb. Ask what they think they might find out from the book.
- Point out that this is an information book. Ask what features they expect to find in the book e.g. contents, glossary, index. Give them a few minutes to find these features. Discuss the purpose and organisation of them.
- Ask children to use the contents to find the chapter called *The ancient world of myths*.

Understand and apply reading strategies

- Read pp2–9 aloud. Demonstrate how to summarise the information given in these pages by identifying the main ideas.
- Ask questions that involve the children in scanning to find key words and phrases e.g. When did the classical age start and end? What is an epic poem?